S. Rivers

Mending Your Broken Heart

Hustle 101

Motivational Speakers & Mentoring Program

Proven Life Changers

Mending your broken heart

Copyright © 2022 by Santiego Rivers

ISBN 978-1-7376037-9-5

I can tell you a lot about love because I know a lot about pain. I struggled with loving myself, which led me to be in relationships with people who found it easier to use me instead of helping me discover my inner self.

I was caught in a vicious cycle that haunted me for years. A broken heart and a lifetime of scars are all I have to show for my heartache and years of pain.

I wanted more when it came to love, so I had to learn to do more to get the desired results. But, unfortunately for me, my way of doing things was not working in my best interest. So, I needed to make a change.

Whether we are trying to love ourselves or love someone else, there is one thing for sure; it will take everything we have inside to get everything we want out of love.

(When it comes to love, I want it all)

From the heartache to the joy, even back to the pain because I will do whatever it takes to get back to having the love I desire.

Me fixing my broken heart could be the same thing you need to do to mend your broken heart.

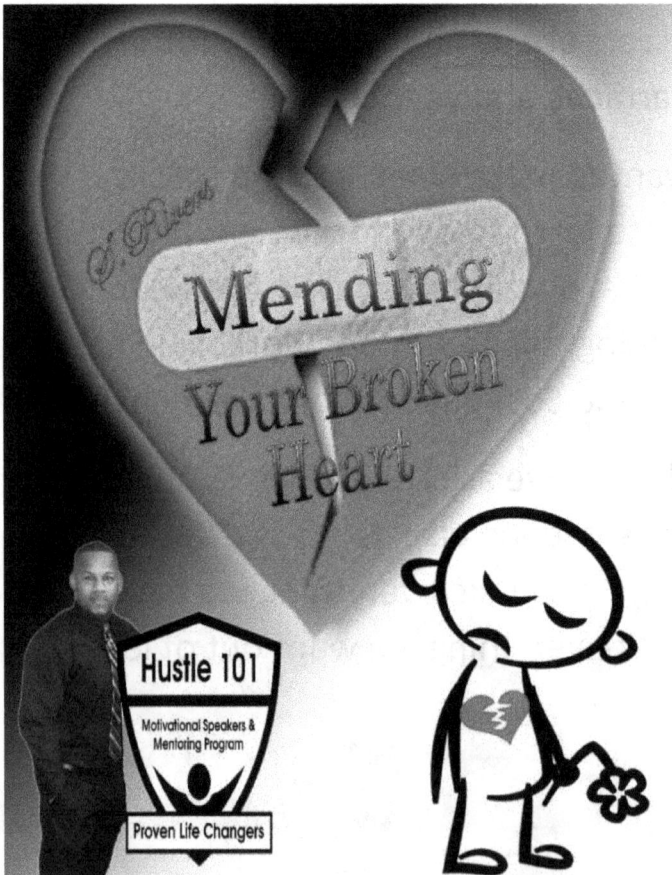

When it comes to love...

My heart has been torn into tiny pieces and scattered on the floor on numerous occasions, but I am still standing.

I am still present, ready to take on whatever comes my way because I have learned the hard way that you will have to take the path less traveled to reach the desired destination when it comes to getting what you want out of life.

I want to be happy!

I **want** to smile as if I have never known sadness, and I **want** to love as if I have never known pain.

It took me a while to learn that I needed first to satisfy my **needs** to have these **wants** that I desire fulfilled.

I had to learn how to mend my broken heart.

To suffer/to grow

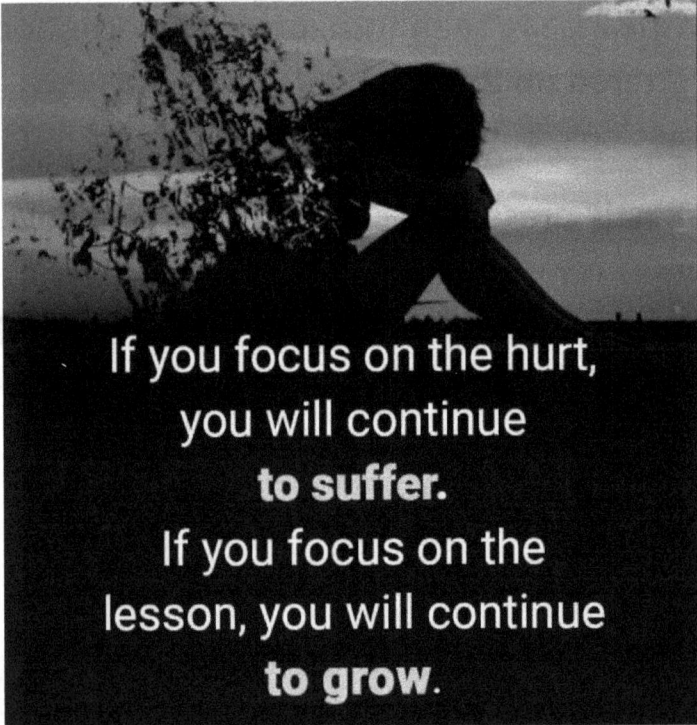

If you focus on the hurt, you will continue **to suffer.** If you focus on the lesson, you will continue **to grow**.

Mending your broken hearts will require you to focus on the lessons you need to learn to grow from instead of the pain that the situation caused you.

We have all experienced a level of pain that we thought that we would never live through, but **we are still here!**

We are survivors!

We have survived moments in our lives that we thought would take our lives, if even by our own hands or reckless actions.

I am not telling you what I think; I am sharing what I know and what I fight daily to keep those thoughts and feelings at bay.

To those who share the same feelings and thoughts, we relive/ carry the pain that the circumstances caused us to bear instead of being alive and learning from the situation we faced.

How many times will it take you to finally decide to change how you are currently doing something that is not working for your best interest?

Change is the only certainty in life. Any person unwilling to change will always be at war with themselves.

We are our worst enemy, but we can be all the help we need to overcome our troubles.

THERE ARE PLENTY OF DIFFICULT OBSTACLES IN YOUR PATH. DON'T ALLOW YOURSELF TO BECOME ONE OF THEM

For those people like me

In our mind, we replay those sad and hurtful moments in our life like our favorite love song, which leaves us caught in the moment.

We relive all our **could, would**, and **should** have moments that we could never change or should try to do. Therefore, everything that happens in life happens for a reason.

I am not saying that we should want or accept all the terrible moments we encounter in life. However, I have grown to understand one thing that has helped give me peace of mind when I am in the eye of the storm.

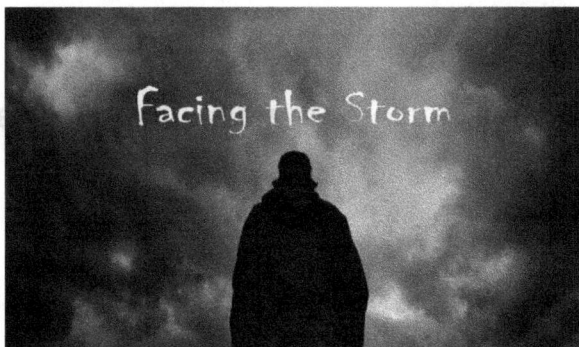

Facing the Storm

Our understanding will never be greater than that of the Most High God

As I stated earlier, everything that happens in our life happens for a reason. Therefore, our understanding will never be

greater than the reasoning of the Most High God.

Believe me when I tell you that I had fought against this reasoning because of my **anger** and **pride** for a very long time without any success. Finally, however, my pursuit of **love** and **happiness** would allow me to learn even when I hated learning that valuable lesson.

What I have learned despite my anger and my pride

Love is present even where there is pain, but our **pride** will always keep happiness out of our life.

You must sacrifice your pride to obtain happiness in your life!

Sometimes you have to sacrifice your pride to really go after what you want - Danielle Brooks

JnSQuotes.In

To get to where I am currently at in my life, I have cried many nights and even mornings.

I have repeated this cycle for a very long time, but I am determined to make my tears of pain turn into tears of joy.

When it comes to my heart being broken by the people I love, I will no longer allow them to take everything they hate about themselves out on me.

I will have more *self-respect* for myself than to allow anyone else to *disrespect* me and the feelings in my heart.

My heart has been broken once too often for my liking. As a result, I have expectations for other people who want to be a part of my life.

The words that I am sorry, I was wrong, I apologize, I will do better must be followed by the actions that I will do whatever it takes to make the relationship work!

I am a big advocate for couple counseling.

When it comes to what I am demanding from myself and other people, my happiness requires action and not words from all parties involved.

I have been through the worse, which reassures me that I will be okay in the end. Of course, I may get bruised a lot, but this I know for sure when it comes to me.

NOT EASILY BROKEN

Coming from what I have been through makes my heart and soul tough, but they are both still ready for love. Therefore, what I have left from everything I have been through and lost is me, and I will make that enough.

I am learning how to love myself, which is good enough for me!

Learning to love me despite the hurt and pain I allowed other people to burden my heart and soul with was not always easy for me to do, but it was worth the effort and the time involved in my growth.

My change and growth were not easy, but it was definitely worth the struggle.

> Wise men change, fools stay the same.
>
> Kevin Gates
>
> www.idlehearts.com

The things that were difficult for me to speak about in my life found their way into my writing which eventually allowed me the opportunity to face my demons and mend my broken heart. My writing helped me find my voice, allowing me to start healing my broken heart.

What is fueling you to start your process of mending your heart?

We all must find a reason to start anything important in our lives, or we'll never finish it, especially when times get hard.

There will always be more reasons to quit/give up while chasing your dreams or simply trying to repair your heart after a setback or significant loss.

As an educator, I would have my scholars write down three things that will motivate them to give their best effort in class each day.

I wanted them to have a visual to remind them why they were giving their best effort and why they would fight through all the negative things that would typically make them quit in their pursuit of achieving greatness.

I then explained that creating a Motivation Visual Board could also help them outside the classroom and in their daily lives if they applied the meaning and the concept.

The meaning and the concept were simple. Each day we must find/ determine why we won't give up amid adversity in our lives.

Whatever you allow driving you/ guide you will succeed at one thing. Either it will guarantee your success or be the reason that you fail.

> **FAILING TO PLAN**
> **=**
> **PLANNING TO FAIL**

Those who focus on the pain instead of the lesson meant to be taught when pain occurs have a hard time moving forward from their current situation, which allows them to be stuck in a predicament longer than intended.

We must constantly remind ourselves that it was not the intended destination when we face heartache.

We wanted love, but unfortunately, heartache and pain will forever be present on the path to love.

There will be setbacks the closer we get to achieving anything we want. Just like you will have to do, I had to determine if I would quit or keep pushing forward?

I had to determine if my legacy would highlight my fears or my willingness to change and grow? After thinking about the question for a while, I decided that I wanted my legacy to be about growth and change, so I needed to change.

Change is the only certainty in life. Either you will change for the best or allow the current situation to change you in ways that you no longer recognize the person staring at you in the mirror.

I did not want my legacy to be about how fear and pain could destroy something meant to be so beautiful. **(Love)**

I focused on change in my life for me and not other people.

Here is a five-year review of my life and why I needed to change my direction, starting with my *mindset*.

- **2018,** I was happy with my new wife getting ready for our new life together. I thought that I had finally found the person who saw me, allowing me to embrace being myself.

- **2019,** I started wondering how many *red flags* I painted white when it came to my new wife and our happy life together? I started thinking that maybe I was trying to satisfy my wants instead of fulfilling my needs. **(There is a difference)** A big difference

- **2020**, We were now facing a significant outbreak! We had to adjust to our new world thanks to *Covid 19*. But, unfortunately, we were not able to get the help that our relationship needed to survive. **(Counseling)**

- **2021**, We were getting a divorce instead of the counseling I desperately wanted for us. I ended my first marriage, and my ex-wife ended her second marriage. Divorce happens when two people fall short of honoring their vows to each other and the Most High God. **(For-better or for-worse)** It takes action to give these words their true meaning!

- **2022**, Come what may, I will be making my comeback because I will put my **wants** and **needs** first, for the first time in my life, and I will not allow pain and heartache to keep me from moving forward. I will be happy starting and ending my journey from inside my heart and soul!

Me making my comeback did not mean that there would not be setbacks and pain along the way. On the contrary, it meant that I had to be willing to face my pain.

The pain, the pain, the pain...

I am talking about that type of pain that makes you want to tear your heart out of your chest and burn it to ashes.

I am talking about the type of pain that makes heaven feel like hell because you feel hurt & alone.

I am talking about the type of pain that would make you want to give up on what you claimed to have always wanted and needed in your life. **(Happiness)**

Pain has taught me that love can hurt like hell, but it can still be gratifying if we respect it and learn from its lesson and not focus on the pain it brings!

Love is the one thing in our life that we try to make sense of, but it does not make any sense.

How can one emotion control every emotion and action in our life?

I have pondered this question for a very long time coming to this conclusion. **I do not know!** So when you find the answer, please let me know!

Trying to fit a square peg into a round peg hole

We are supposed to believe in ourselves and have a positive mindset regardless of the obstacles and adversity we face in life; unfortunately, **I am not there yet**.

We shouldn't allow the opinion of others to control how we think and feel about ourselves; unfortunately for me, **I am not there yet.**

We are supposed to be tougher than we look and not let negative words and actions affect us; unfortunately, **I am not there yet**.

There are many times when I need a moment to reflect on what I am going through and how it is making me feel inside, but to be honest, I need to be by myself to cry.

Men cry; this is something that most boys do not understand.

I have fought back many tears, which made them feel like acid as they ran down my face.

I have gritted my teeth and clenched my fists, telling myself that I will be okay, despite knowing that I am not okay. Trying to fool the world, I only succeeded in fooling myself that the secrets I was holding inside were not showing to others and destroying me from the inside out as I tried to keep something inside of me that I should not have held onto in the first place.

The foolish pride of a **child** turns into the burden/ cross of a **man** that he carries on his back like a sinner-searching for salvation in an unforgiving world filled with Christians.

Jesus Christ!

If God can ease the pain that my mind is causing my heart and soul, take me to church so I can leave all my burdens at the altar.

...You do not have because you do not ask God.

James 4:2

They say that you have not because you asked not; this can't be true for me! Every day, I am on my knees, shouting, pass the stars into heaven for God to please remove these burdens that I bear in my soul, which troubles my heart because I do not want the pain.

It took me a while and many tears to realize that my focus should be more on the lesson than the pain that the lesson was causing me to feel because I was not ready to learn what the lesson was trying to teach me.

I have overcome obstacles that I did not want to face because I learned that not standing up to them or meeting them head-on was worse. I carried the proof that the pain of running from my fears was worse because it showed in my heart.

I knew that it was time to change because it was the only thing I could do.

You will never know how strong you are until being strong is all you have to lean on.

I am there now!

I am ready to mend my broken heart by letting go of everything God never intended for me to carry or hold onto.

I am trying to now walk by faith and not by sight. My eyes have deceived me one too many times.

How many times can I keep crying over the same thing until I finally realize the one thing I need to do is what is best for me to do.

I need to learn how to love myself. Then, everything and everyone else will follow my lead!

The steps of a good man are numbered, so I am counting my blessings and giving God everything that he did not mean for me to worry about.

Let go *and* let God.

I hope that this book allows you to get to where I aim to be in my life. Then, once we both reach that place, we can have a conversation about how the square pegs stopped trying to fit in the round circle and found a way to mend their broken heart that God never intended to be broken.

Our victory will be greater than the pain and the heartache that we had to endure in our life!

You can't have strength without the struggle!

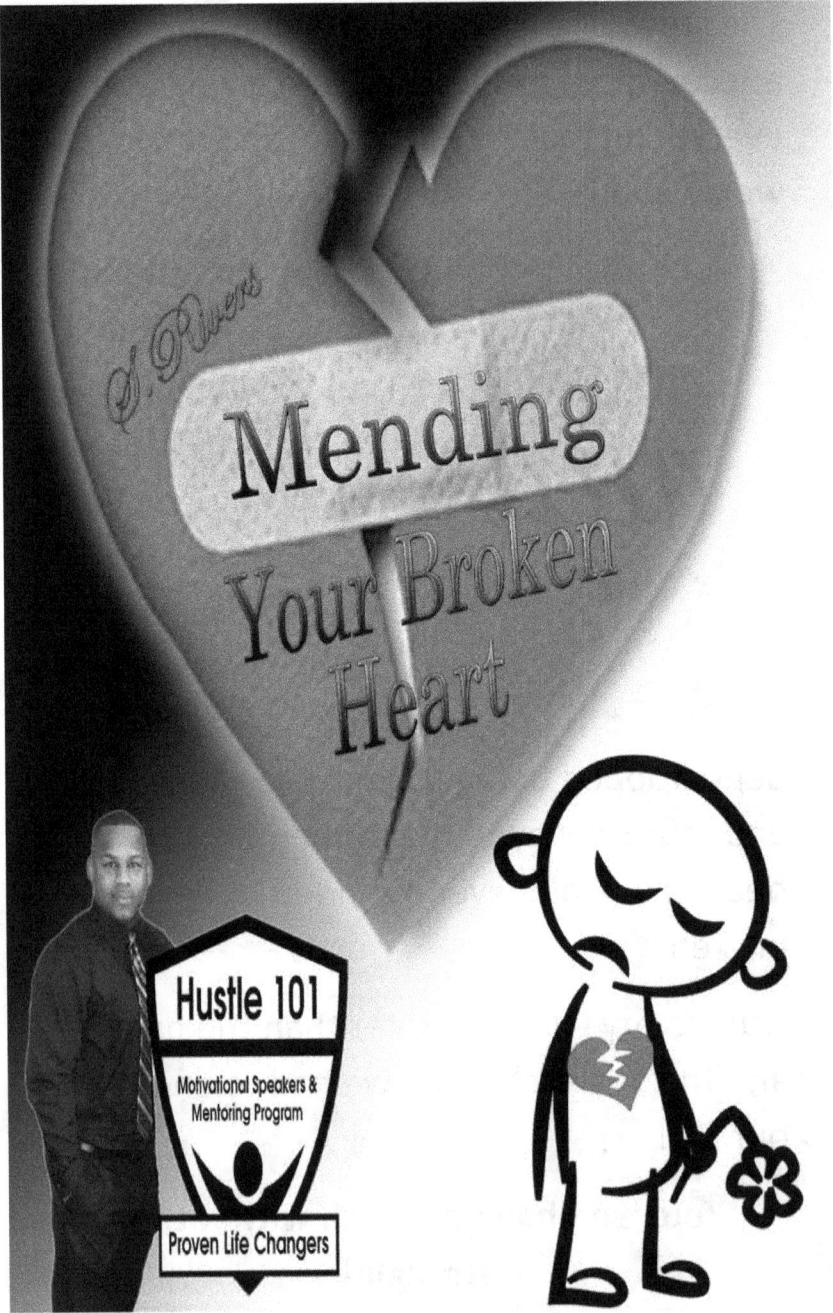

www.ingramcontent.com/pod-product-compliance
Lightning Source LLC
Chambersburg PA
CBHW052143270326
41930CB00012B/2999